# Anna's Day of GRATITUDE

# Anna's Day of GRATITUDE

Written by
**Gail Stevenson**

Illustrated by
**Mary Baker**

My own garden in
Grandfather's special
wheelbarrow! "Oh, thank you,
Daddy," I cry, and I hug him
with gratitude.

I am so excited that I can hardly wait for the first sunny day when I can begin.

LEAVE ROOM IN
your garden
FOR THE
Angels TO
DANCE

Mummy asks me what I am going to call my garden. I am so grateful that I decide to call it "My Garden of Gratitude."

I ask if I can go and tell my best friend, Mary, and Mummy says yes.

I run with my dog MacGregor to Mary's house to tell her. Then we all walk together along the winding path to the ocean.

We see Mrs. Smylie gathering twigs for her fire.
She is old and bent over and walks with a cane.
She lives in the village and is our friend.

Mrs. Smylie says she is grateful for the twigs
because she will be lovely and warm.

How could Mrs. Smylie feel such gratitude
and happiness when she is old and has to
walk with a cane?

Suddenly, it starts to rain. Mary and I want to help Mrs. Smylie, so we carry some of her twigs home. That makes me feel very happy.

When we get there, Mrs. Smylie says she is going to make bread, and if our mothers say yes, then we can help.

We run home to ask, and as quickly as we can, we run back to Mrs. Smylie's warm kitchen.

"Do you know how long it takes to make bread?" she asks.

"A few hours?" Mary asks.

"Well," says Mrs. Smylie, "from the time the wheat is planted until harvest, it takes several seasons."

"Wow, that is an awfully long time for just a loaf of bread," I say.

"Nature takes time and so does the making of bread," says Mrs. Smylie.

While we wait for the yeast to rise, she measures and mixes all the ingredients into the flour. She tells us how wheat grows and how flour is made.

Mrs. Smylie sets the table with tea cups and plates. She makes Mary and me cambric tea and she cuts slices of bread and spreads them with butter and jam.

"We need to give thanks for all that we have," says Mrs. Smylie. So together we say,

"Thank you for the world so sweet,
thank you for the food we eat,
thank you for the birds that sing,
thank you, God, for everything."

At the end of the day, Mrs. Smylie gives us each a loaf of bread, and we go home to our cottages for dinner.

# Song*

rbuthnot

ood friends
gs too,
ether
 through.

ighter
ny ears
mories
 the years.

d, so grateful,
to see and do.
d, so grateful.
nuch better
happy
teful too.

Rainbows and sunsets
so beautifully drawn
promise tomorrow
before they are gone.

Sun-kissed clouds at sunrise
like paintings in the sky,
the things that make
the magic in our lives.

Chorus

I'm so happy, so glad, so grateful,
for beautiful things to see and do.
I'm so happy, so glad, so grateful,
and all we share together
makes me happy and so
grateful too.

*Available on iTunes

# Gail Stevenson

Gail Stevenson was born and raised in Vancouver, where she met and married her husband, Ken, and raised a family. She has had careers in construction and retail and is still involved in the development business.

Gail is the author of four books, including *The Time of In Between*, an anthology of the seasons of our lives, and the co-author of *The Autumn Ring*. *Anna's Day of Gratitude* is her first children's book, inspired by the promise of another generation. She has four children, thirteen grandchildren and one great-granddaughter. Gail now lives in Qualicum Beach on Vancouver Island, B.C.

# Mary Baker

Mary Baker is a recognized, widely exhibited artist educated in art history and creative writing. She has sold her work in commercial galleries and in solo, group and private exhibitions in galleries in West Vancouver over the past three decades. In 2010, Mary created illustrations for a book by Grace Chen, a young woman with Down's syndrome.

Mary illustrated the children's book *A Giraffe Called Geranium*, published in 2014, written by Ainslie Manson, which was nominated for a Chocolate Lily Book Prize. Mary now lives in Roberts Creek, B.C.

CPSIA information can be obtained at www.ICGtesting.com
Printed in the USA
BVIW12n1936021017
496492BV00003B/3

# UP AND AWAY

# Ways to use Up and Away

This book contains carefully devised activities which help develop important early learning skills. There is no order to the activities. You can read the story first or try the questions as you read.

## Words

Some questions encourage your child to discuss the story and think about the characters. You can extend the questions to talk about their own experiences. For example, have they seen a ladybird? Do they remember going to a market?

## Maths

Some questions explore number, size, shape and colour. Try expanding these activities: How many yellow things can you find on a page?

## Science

Some questions encourage observation and understanding of the natural world and technology. Try talking about experiences your child may have had too.

## Time and place

Questions about the map at the end of the book invite you to work out the journey in the story and to notice how details have changed. In this way children can explore early concepts of geography and history.

Kingfisher Books, Grisewood & Dempsey Ltd
Elsley House, 24-30 Great Titchfield Street, London W1P 7AD

First published in 1994 by Kingfisher Books
2 4 6 8 10 9 7 5 3 1

Copyright © Colin and Moira Maclean 1994

Educational consultant: Jane Salt
Designed by Caroline Johnson

BRITISH LIBRARY CATALOGUING IN PUBLICATION DATA
A catalogue record for this book is available from the British Library

ISBN 1 85697 178 3

Phototypeset by Southern Positives and Negatives (SPAN),
Lingfield, Surrey
Printed and bound in Spain

KINGFISHER
# Story Activity Books

# UP AND AWAY

Written and illustrated by
Colin and Moira Maclean

Kingfisher Books

James leaned on the windowsill and watched the
people passing below. There was Laura skipping up
the street. James waved and called, "Hello."

Laura looked up. "I saw a bloobaloo," she called.
"A great big bloobaloo."

"A what?" shouted James.

But Laura went skipping on and by the time James had run downstairs she had gone.

What had she said? A bloobaloo! But what was a bloobaloo? Whatever it was, James had to see one.

- Can you see who is wearing these shoes?

- What do you think the dog wants to do?

- What do you think this ladder is for?

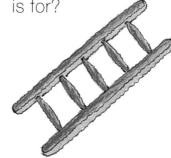

- Who is carrying these tiles?

- Can you see who is wearing this coat?

- Can you see people carrying other things in the street?

In the market square James found people selling fruit and fish and cups and vases but nothing that looked like a bloobaloo. "Has anyone seen a bloobaloo?" he asked but everyone was too busy to listen. Only the big bird on a perch heard his question.

"Bloo-bloo-blooey … what … what … what?" it cackled.

• Point to all the fruit you can see. Which do you like to eat?

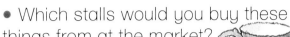

• Which stalls would you buy these things from at the market?

• What would you like to buy at the market?

James went on. In the next street people were putting furniture into a removal lorry.

"We're moving to a new house," said a boy with freckles. James helped him carry a huge plant. "Is this a bloobaloo plant?" he asked.

"I don't think so," said the boy with freckles. "What's a bloobaloo?"

- How many things outside the house have wheels?

- Can you find these ones outside the house?

- Which thing has two wheels?

- Which things have four wheels?

Around the corner, James came to the bridge and stopped to look down at the water. There was a boat chugging along the canal and on the boat a woman was busy hanging out washing. Her dog barked and she looked up and waved.

"Have you seen a bloobaloo?" called James.

The woman nodded and pointed. Then the boat chugged on its way beneath the bridge.

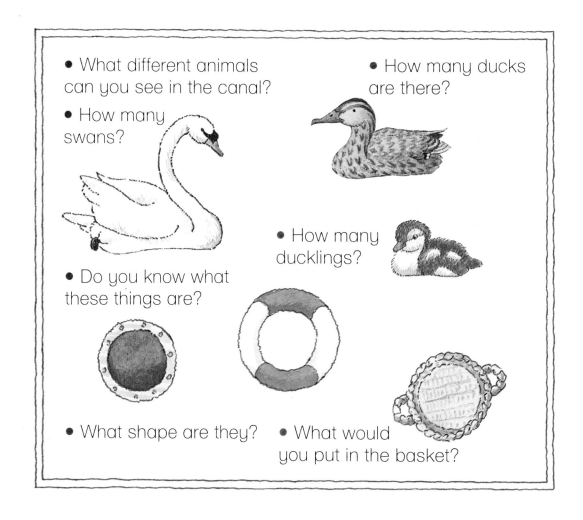

• What different animals can you see in the canal?

• How many swans?

• How many ducks are there?

• How many ducklings?

• Do you know what these things are?

• What shape are they?

• What would you put in the basket?

James rushed off up the road and found three people working in an old house. Was there a bloobaloo here? James stopped to look. One man was mending a broken wall. Another was joining up some pipes. A woman was fitting new planks into the floor.

"Would you pass me that hammer as you're standing there," she said.

James took it to her. "Is that a bloobaloo?" he asked, pointing to a huge bulgy thing in the corner.

"A bloobaloo?" said the woman in a puzzled voice. "No, not that. It's just the old water tank."

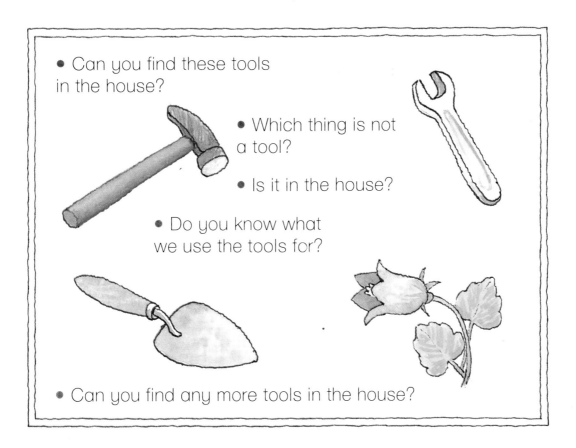

- Can you find these tools in the house?

- Which thing is not a tool?

- Is it in the house?

- Do you know what we use the tools for?

- Can you find any more tools in the house?

James was disappointed. He still hadn't found a bloobaloo. He walked on but his legs were getting tired and he sat down at the side of the road to have a rest. He heard a rustling noise behind him. I wonder if that's a bloobaloo, he thought.

• Look for these flowers in the grass.

• Which one has four petals?

• Which one has five petals?

Suddenly, something bounded out of the grass.
Was it the bloobaloo? No – it was just a rabbit!
It stared at James, twitched its whiskers and
disappeared with a flick of white tail.

- Can you spot these bugs hiding in the grass.

- Which is the smallest?

- Which is the biggest?

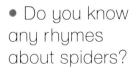

- Do you know any rhymes about spiders?

James was fed up. Did Laura really say bloobaloo? Maybe there wasn't such a thing. Maybe he should go home. He started to kick stones along the road. Then bump! he banged into someone.

"Hey!" said a man leading a horse and cart. "Where are you off to, my lad?"

"I'm looking for a bloobaloo," said James sadly, "but I can't find one anywhere."

The man looked puzzled, then he smiled.

"Keep going," he said. "Just follow the path around my farm."

- What can you see in the farmer's sacks?

- How many sacks are in the cart?

- How many ducks are in the pond?

- Where do you think the farmer is going?

Drip! Drip! Drip! It was starting to rain. James raced down the path and dived under the roof of a shed to shelter.

- Look for these animals in the farmyard.

- Which animal goes oink oink?

- What noises do the other animals make?

- Do you know what a baby hen is called?

- What are other baby animals called?

"Brrrr!" he shivered. Then the back
of his neck prickled. In the darkness
behind him something big was breathing.

Had the baloobaloo found him? James
yelled and whirled round. But it wasn't a
bloobaloo. It was a friendly calf trying to
lick his hair. James stroked its nose until
the rain stopped, then set off along the
farm path.

And at last James saw it. The bloobaloo. It was ... of course it was ... a blue balloon. The most enormous, gigantic, stupendous bluest balloon James had ever seen. He ran towards it, waving his arms. He ran and ran.

"You're just in time," said the man in the basket. "Come for a ride."

And when the bloobaloo had taken them up and away, James looked down at the ground far below. He could see all the places he'd been that morning.

Can you see the places too on the map?